essential care

A CAREER AS A
SOCIAL MEDIA
MANAGER

JEFF MAPUA

Rosen
YA
New York

Published in 2018 by The Rosen Publishing Group, Inc.
29 East 21st Street, New York, NY 10010

First Edition

Library of Congress Cataloging-in-Publication Data

Names: Mapua, Jeff, author.
Title: A career as a social media manager / Jeff Mapua.
Description: New York : Rosen Publishing, 2018 | Series: Essential careers
| Audience: Grades 7–12. | Includes bibliographical references and index.
Identifiers: LCCN 2017013077 | ISBN 9781538381489 (library bound) | ISBN
9781508178736 (pbk.)
Subjects: LCSH: Career development--Juvenile literature. | Social media—
Management—Juvenile literature.
Classification: LCC HF5381 .M316 2018 | DDC 302.23/1023--dc23
LC record available at https://lccn.loc.gov/2017013077

Manufactured in China

contents

INTRO

A customer bites into a Quesalupa during Taco Bell's Blind Order Bash campaign. Companies such as Taco Bell use social media to their advantage and create enthusiasm for upcoming products or services.

DUCTION

In February 2016, Taco Bell had a new item it wanted to unveil. The fast-food restaurant company already offered a large menu. How could it introduce something new that people would find exciting? The company decided to utilize social media to its advantage. It announced a "first-ever, blind pre-order" campaign, according to tech journalist James A. Martin. Taco Bell used Twitter and Snapchat along with television advertisements that ran during the Super Bowl to let people know about the product. Customers could order Taco Bell's new, mystery item online. They had one day to pick up their item between 2:00 p.m. and 4:00 p.m. at their local Taco Bell restaurants. As Martin reported, the Blind Pre-Order Bash was designed to create excitement. Taco Bell hoped its plan would work.

The strategy was a big success. Taco Bell was able to create "pent-up desire" for the new Quesalupa. This anticipation was created by giving the company's biggest fans early or exclusive access to a new product. It almost did not matter what the item was. The success was the result of a great social media plan. Companies have people who focus on running social media accounts. Taco Bell's social media manager and social media team played a big part in making their company a profit.

Social media was not always a part of life. Considering how popular social media is today, it is sometimes easy to forget that there was a time when Facebook was just a website for college students at a few select schools. Before the era of Twitter, celebrities and public figures had no way to interact with fans and the general population at any time of the day or night. Telling someone to "like a photo" or "unfollow a user" would have been met with a look of confusion. Yet, in a short amount of time, social media has grown very quickly. Social media has branched out beyond groups of friends. It became a way to conduct business. Companies around the world had to evolve to keep up with its popularity and business potential.

Social media became an effective way for a business to provide customer service. Using this approach, a business could answer questions publicly. In addition, a company could engage with its customers to establish trust and to sort out problems. Interacting with the public and a company's customers through social media, though, requires leadership and organization. Without proper guidance and rules, a company could easily say the wrong thing for all to see. Because of this need for direction and control over its social media pages, a business will require a social media manager.

Social media has changed people's lives. It also is transforming the world of business. Taco Bell would most likely agree to its advantages in the realm of marketing and advertising. For those interested in social media, a career as a social media manager might be the perfect fit for them today and for years to come.

chapter 1

A SOCIAL MEDIA MANAGER'S PROFESSION

As businesses learn to adopt the latest platforms, more opportunities to make social media a profession have become available. It sounds like a dream job for those many young people who already consider themselves experts in the field. However, what are the general tasks? What does a social media manager do exactly? Is a career as a social media manager right for them?

THE BASICS

At the core of the social media manager profession is communication. Communication is done through online platforms that allow people to share content. There are various social networks available today to anyone with an internet connection. These include Facebook, Snapchat, Tumblr, Instagram, Twitter, Google+, and many more. There are many platforms targeted to people outside of the United States, too. These include Baidu Tieba in China, Vkontakte in Russia, and Taringa in Latin America.

One of the major goals of a social media manager is to help build a company's brand reputation. The landscape of active platforms can vary month to month. The platforms are only as successful as the strength and activity of their audience. If a platform has a million users but only a small fraction of those are engaged, then it is not a strong platform. The major

Social networks such as Facebook and LinkedIn created applications for smartphones and other mobile devices. The networks are available to users at any time of the day.

players, such as Facebook, have millions of users active every day. A social media manager needs to be aware of which sites customers use and which ones they ignore.

A manager runs the employer's social media accounts and creates content to post online. Content can take many different shapes. It can be an image, a text, a video, an audio clip, or any combination of these forms. It is designed to make people interested in a business or brand. A well-made image can get people talking about a company's product or service. These conversations are managed by the social media manager. Perhaps a hashtag on Twitter could gain popularity. Social media managers could find ways to jump into the conversation to increase awareness of their brand.

THE DAY-TO-DAY DUTIES

Social media managers do more than just post content. Every company is different and will ask its social media managers to complete tasks that suit the company's specific needs. Companies with many employees could ask their social media managers to focus on only managing their brand. At smaller companies, being the social media manager may just be part of an employee's job.

Monitoring a company's online activity and conversations about the company can be a very formidable task. Depending on the size of the company, there could be hundreds or thousands of tweets, posts, and shares every day. A social media manager must constantly keep up with what is going on in the world. It can be an all-consuming responsibility and take up time outside of the office, too. Some people may find that kind of work fun, exciting, and challenging. Two more significant duties involve creation of a marketing funnel and managing customer service and brand reputation.

Digital marketing professionals, such as this senior marketing adviser, are responsible for managing their company's social media accounts, online reputations, and digital marketing strategies. They reply to customer questions and complaints.

MARKETING FUNNEL CREATION

The term "marketing funnel" means the process of moving a person from learning about a product or service to the purchase of that product or service. Getting someone to buy a company's product begins first by making that person aware that the product exists. That important first step is up to the social media manager. He or she must create a daily presence of the product in the lives of current and prospective customers. Customers must associate the company's brand with the product. This concept is called brand presence or awareness. It is a form of soft selling. One method of soft selling focuses on building a relationship with a customer rather than focusing on the product. Another technique is telling personal stories to make the product more appealing to the potential customer on an emotional level.

People who interact with a brand or company online are part of the marketing funnel. They are in the process of

THE DIGITAL MARKETING FUNNEL
GROW YOUR SALES AND ATTRACT NEW CUSTOMERS

1 AWARENESS

2 CONSIDERATION

3 PURCHASE

4 RETENTION

5 ADVOCACY

ATTRACT

CONVERT

ENGAGE

SELL

CONNECT

MARKETING AND STATISTICS

Lorem ipsum dolor sit amet, consectetur adipiscing elit, sed do eiusmod tempor incididunt ut labore et dolore magna aliqua. Ut enim ad minim veniam, quis nostrud exercitation ullamco laboris nisi ut aliquip ex ea commodo consequat. Duis aute irure dolor in reprehenderit in voluptate velit esse cillum dolore eu fugiat nulla pariatur. Excepteur sint occaecat cupidatat non proident, sunt in culpa qui officia deserunt mollit anim id est laborum.

Lorem ipsum dolor sit amet, consectetur adipiscing elit, sed do eiusmod tempor incididunt ut labore et dolore magna aliqua. Ut enim ad minim veniam, quis nostrud exercitation ullamco laboris nisi ut aliquip ex ea commodo consequat. Duis aute irure dolor in reprehenderit in voluptate velit esse cillum dolore eu fugiat nulla pariatur. Excepteur sint occaecat cupidatat non proident, sunt in culpa qui officia deserunt mollit anim id est laborum.

ITEM 1
ITEM 2
ITEM 3
ITEM 4

25%   **50%**

CHART NUMBER 1   CHART NUMBER 2

SALES INCREASE

MARKETING STRATEGIES

Social media managers help their companies add potential customers to their marketing funnels. They help people become aware of their products, then eventually turn them into customers.

purchasing a product or service. Technology has provided social media managers with tools that collect data and contact information of these potential customers. This information can then be used to make more people a part of the marketing funnel.

CUSTOMER SERVICE AND BRAND REPUTATION MANAGER

Social media managers are also customer service representatives. People often share experiences that they have had with a company online. Their friends and family will hear about both good and bad experiences. Using advanced tools such as Klout a social media manager can monitor what people are saying about their company online. The manager must help resolve an angry customer's problem. Responding quickly and with kindness can go a long way in helping a brand's image.

BENEFIT TO BUSINESS

Social media supports business functions such as public relations, marketing, sales lead generation, customer service, and market research. Sales lead generation refers to the process of finding people whom a salesperson can contact to make a sale.

One of the common measurements used to determine how useful something is to a business is called return on investment (ROI). A business invests in things it believes will help increase profits, such as a new sign to hang outside a store or upgraded internet service. The ROI shows how much that new sign or upgraded internet service benefited the company financially. Social media is a similar tool in which organizations invest.

There are many ways to measure how useful social media is to a company. These include the number of website visitors, the number of Facebook fans or Twitter followers, a change in

FOR THE FAMOUS

One career path for a social media manager is representing a public figure or celebrity. Having a social media presence is essential for any actor, musician, politician, or other type of performer. The use of social media has become so important that it has grown from letting people know about an upcoming show to helping a celebrity get elected to public office. Rather than reading about what a famous person is doing through articles or interviews, celebrities can communicate directly to their fans.

Public figures may choose to let someone else run their accounts. Some, such as New York City mayor Bill de Blasio, hire a single person. Others, such as actress Emma Watson, hire a company with dozens of employees to run their accounts. These social media managers are sometimes given general guidelines about what they can and cannot post online. For example, some celebrities want their accounts to avoid controversial topics, such as politics or religion. Others ask their managers only to promote the latest project they are working on, such as a movie or new album. Some must get approval from the account owner for every single item that they share. The position can be fulfilling and is described as a "dream job" by some. However, in cases like that of the social media manager for the mayor of New York City, according to senior writer Josh Duboff of *Vanity Fair,* that dream job turned into a bad dream because of the very long work hours and having to get the go-ahead on all postings, including his own personal accounts.

the number of visitors to a store, or the number of comments on a post. Examples of outcomes that involve finances include the shifting of customer service costs to Twitter, a change in revenue from sales, or the number of sales made from new customers that have been gained through Facebook. Financial

Although many people see social media as a way to connect with friends and family online, businesses use social media networks as tools to increase their profits.

and nonfinancial gains cannot be compared to each other. However, both can be used to find out how successful social media is to a company. In other words, measurements such as these can determine social media's ROI.

IS IT THE RIGHT FIT?

Social media is a fairly recent addition to the business world. Businesses continue to figure out what roles are necessary for the successful application of social media. Job titles and duties can be vague, for example, idea inventor, social media guru, or social media czar are some titles used in the industry. People in the industry frequently have to figure out for themselves what exactly their roles are for the company.

Choosing a career in social media means being able to complete a variety of tasks—from interacting with customers to writing content for a website. It also means communicating well with many people. Social media managers must remain in control of their emotions when confronted with an angry or dissatisfied consumer online. This career also can mean using the newest technology that is changing the world.

chapter 2

SKILLS AND TRAITS FOR SUCCESS

What skills do accomplished social media managers share? Not all social media managers perform the same tasks. However, there are some abilities that they must all possess. There also are personality traits that help social media managers succeed in their roles. Finally, what skills and traits do employers look for when interviewing and hiring for a position as a social media manager? Knowing what these skills and traits are could be the difference between landing a job and going back to searching the job boards.

SKILLS AND COMPETENCIES

Everyone has at least one skill that they come to naturally. Other skills require patience and practice to master. Excelling at a profession, particularly one like that of social media manager, requires learning specific skills. On which skills should developing social media managers concentrate most of their efforts?

CUSTOMER SERVICE

Having a customer-first mind-set is a skill that can be developed over time. If a customer posts a complaint online or asks a question, that individual will appreciate receiving a quick response. A social media manager must monitor all social media channels to make sure customers are not ignored. If the customer's issue requires extra attention, a social media manager could then move the conversation to a mode of communication that is more private, such as email or a phone call.

No matter what happens, a social media manager must always remain professional. This means avoiding arguments online. Professional social media managers must respond to messages in a way that helps their company and brand. Responses must be part of a company's social media strategy. For example, social media managers may try to mention a new product or service.

GRAPHICS PRODUCTION

Research has shown that people prefer their internet content to have pictures. Articles with images get 94 percent more views online than articles without images, according to digital entrepreneur Jeff Bullas, as reported by Jayson DeMers on Forbes.com. Bullas also states that tweets with images are clicked on 18 percent more than text-only tweets. On Facebook, there is an amazing 120 percent increase in engagement for posts with photos over posts without them. According to media professionals, for businesses that want to attract women, millennials, and teens images are even more essential. This type of image targeting is particularly important on social media platforms such as Instagram and Pinterest that rely on images for their content.

Because of the necessity and merits of using images, social media managers could benefit from learning graphics production skills. These skills include being able to create, design, and edit images for social media sites to attract a large audience. A good strategy, too, is to learn to use graphics tools such as Photoshop.

Research shows that images are key to better engagement from users with content online. Social media managers should be skilled in the use of image editing programs.

WRITING SKILLS

Social media managers are communicators. Because most social media sites rely on text posts, social media managers must have good writing skills. They must be able to express thoughts and the messages that the company wishes to circulate. In addition, communicating with customers online is done primarily in writing, such as for review sites like Yelp and applications like Instagram. Written communication must stay on topic, and the writer's tone must be professional.

SEARCH ENGINE OPTIMIZATION EXPERIENCE

Search engine optimization (SEO) has quickly become an important part of any company that conducts business online. Search engines such as Google and Bing make it easy for people to find information that they want. These search engines use complicated formulas, called algorithms, to determine which results to show users. SEO is a way for a website to make itself more likely to appear in the list of results after a search on Google or Bing. For example, if a person searches for restaurants that are located nearby, the restaurants that do not appear in the search results will miss out on a customer. Restaurant owners depend on their social media managers to make their websites more visible to search engines.

Social media managers must understand how search engines work. Using that knowledge, they can help make their company's website more visible.

HELPFUL TRAITS

Traits are different from skills. Traits are qualities that differentiate one person from another. They are related to a person's personality and character. Like skills, traits also can be developed. There are several traits that have proven to be beneficial for those who work in the social media field.

nks
ilding

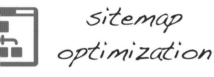

sitemap
optimization

software
development

HTML

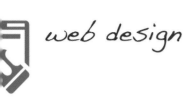
web design

dback

This diagram shows some of the main marketing elements involved in the search engine optimization (SEO) process. SEO has quickly become an essential part of social media and advertising.

REAL JOB POSTS

The requirements for social media managers have changed since the position first came about. Businesses have learned more about what works and what does not. They now have a better idea about what type of person would make a good social media manager. There are many social media manager jobs available today. Looking at what companies want can be helpful when trying to find the perfect fit.

One large museum in the United States, for instance, looked for a social media manager who was an experienced user of multiple social media platforms. The museum required someone who had managed accounts for an organization. They also wanted someone able to use Photoshop and word processing applications. Many employers look for experience in web development, such as in HTML and Dreamweaver, a popular website creation tool.

A company that sells tea looked for someone with a positive attitude and who was interested in learning new skills. The company wanted someone who had good communication skills, was detailed oriented, and worked quickly.

POSSESSES A PASSION FOR SOCIAL MEDIA

Having passion for a profession is paramount to flourishing in that field. A passionate person not only will enjoy the job more, but he or she will also have a better chance at achieving success. A passionate social media manager is one who enjoys participating in various forms of online interactions. People can tell the difference between a social media account run by a passionate person and one managed by someone who is just doing it for a job.

Successful social media managers have great enthusiasm for social media and are interested in participating in online interactions outside of work.

Passionate social media managers also make themselves available at all times. Being accessible is an important characteristic to have in a job in which customers and clients can make contact at any time. Status updates are read at all hours. Much of the workday falls outside of working hours. Lost time means lost opportunities.

STAYS INFORMED

Successful managers keep themselves informed about what is going on in the industry. They read various websites, blogs, and articles that share news about the latest trends in social media. Sites such as TechCrunch and Social Media Today, among others, keep readers up to date about the latest tools and mobile technology. Social media moves very quickly. If managers fail to pay attention, they could soon find themselves missing opportunities. For example, if a social media tool releases an important upgrade or update, a business will need it or it could fall behind its competitors.

IS A CRITICAL THINKER

Social media managers must be able to solve a variety of problems quickly. Customers contact a business for numerous reasons. The social media manager who is responsible for responding to these customers will encounter all types of problems. Many problems will be unique. Their solutions will need to be equally unique. Critical thinking—objectively and carefully analyzing problems

Becoming a social media manager usually requires having previous experience with online campaigns and content creation.

and assumptions to form solid judgments—is essential for a social media manager's success in his or her career.

Social media managers must also be able to figure out how to reach the largest number of people with their content. Managers must determine what type of content their customers like the best or if a certain type of social media campaign is more popular than another. There are analytical tools that provide social media managers with data that answer these questions. However, it is up to the person and his or her critical thinking to make decisions based on the available information.

WHAT EMPLOYERS WANT

Most employers want their social media managers to have previous social media experience. Being a frequent Facebook user is not enough experience. Employers prefer to hire people who have managed and implemented social media campaigns already. It used to be possible to have a social media team that was light on experience, but that is no longer the case. Social media has evolved since its early days, and social media managers must be able to take advantage of various opportunities to have the desired effects for the employers' businesses.

Social advertising experience is an indispensable requirement for many employers. According to Jayson DeMers on Forbes.com, in 2015, 70 percent of marketers planned on increasing the amount of money they spent on advertisements that appear on social media sites. Advertisements can be a photograph with a link to an online store or posts that look like regular content. The social media manager must have the ability to target the advertisements wisely or no one will notice them.

Social media managers also must be willing to balance their online personal and professional lives. Privacy can be a concern, of course, but there are measures that a manager can take to keep important personal information out of the public eye. Managers should refrain from using their personal information, including names and locations, in their business-related tweets and posts. On personal accounts, social media managers are encouraged to deny friend and follow requests from strangers and to keep their privacy settings up to date.

chapter 3

PREPARATION AND EDUCATION

Competition for jobs can be intense, so getting an early start can be extremely helpful. Students who take classes that apply to social media management have an advantage over others who are hoping to enter the field. Education should continue beyond the high school years and into the college years. Even while working as a professional, there are programs available to help further a career as a social media manager.

SOCIAL MEDIA IN HIGH SCHOOL

Some high schools use social media as a learning tool. Beaver Country Day School in Massachusetts, for example, used the popular chat application Skype to speak with students from around the world. The school administrators saw that their students were always on their phones or tablets checking social media. Rather than fight it, they decided to encourage teachers to use social media in their classrooms. Students learned how to use platforms such as Facebook, Twitter, and Pinterest to connect with people. They even connected with doctors at various hospitals to get comments about the accuracy of a website about brain cancer the students had created.

Some high school students study social media itself. Missouri English teacher Beth Phillips explained the social media curriculum she developed in an article on JEADigitalMedia.org. It covers a historical perspective (how social media has influenced how people send and receive information); the social media writing process (examination of users and their integrity); engagement (how to use social media to broaden their social networks); social media writing structure (how to use social media to reach an audience and how to write within media sites' criteria); media analysis (how to investigate how businesses are using social media to sell their products and services); and law and ethics (learning about the legal and appropriate uses of social media). Phillips believes that her curriculum not only teaches students about the technology itself but also instructs them in how to learn the skills they must have to be able to adjust to the developing technologies of the future.

Another way teachers use social media in the classroom is by having students create their own podcasts. A podcast is a digital audio or video recording, usually part of a series, that people download. A podcast can be about anything. For example, some teachers have asked their students to create a podcast about a topic that they are covering in class, such as immigration or the solar system. Students research their topics and then write a script to communicate what they have learned. Afterward, they can post their content online. To take it a step further, they can even promote their podcasts by tweeting out a link to download the episode or share it on Facebook.

MAJORS AND ADVANCED DEGREES

The job of social media manager typically requires a bachelor's degree. After high school, potential social media managers

These high school students are working on a podcast with the help of a college student (back row left). With the rise of podcasting and its use in marketing and social media, many high schools are including lessons about such technology and its proper use in their curricula.

must decide on their focus of study in college. Social media degree programs are still relatively new in higher education. For colleges and universities that do not offer a specific degree in social media, there are options that can provide the appropriate training and education. There are also master's degree–level programs available to further one's studies.

UNDERGRADUATE STUDIES

There are several communications-related majors students can pursue on their way to a career in social media management. Subjects such as public relations, communications, and journalism can help prepare students for the working world. Employers look to hire job candidates with degrees in communications, journalism, or marketing.

Public relations is about creating and maintaining a favorable public image for a company, organization, or famous person. Attaining a public relations degree requires taking classes in communications, ethics, management, and marketing. A degree in communications has many uses. Communications majors can go on to a variety of career paths, including law, television, education, and human resources. Useful classes for a social media manager are visual communications, web design, video journalism, and media graphics. Journalism majors pursue careers in diverse media, such as in television, print media, or photojournalism. Many of these areas involve some type of writing, such as newspaper reporting. Today social media management is a popular option for those with journalism degrees. Core courses required for a journalism degree include ethics, reporting, understanding media, and digital skills. Marketing degrees help students learn about promoting and selling products to consumers. Courses relevant to social media managers include communications, marketing principles, business principles, and consumer behavior. Marketing majors can go on to hold job titles such as marketing specialist, account manager, and sales manager.

GRADUATE STUDIES

Master's degree programs are generally more focused on a specific topic than undergraduate degrees. For example, a social media specialist for the Smithsonian Institution's National Museum of African American History and Culture in Washington, DC, earned a master's degree in internet marketing.

Some schools offer internet marketing coursework as part of their master of business administration (MBA) programs. Others offer social media studies for students who are pursuing their MBAs. Getting into an MBA program can be very competitive. It generally requires a bachelor's degree, a satisfactory score in the Graduate Management Admission Test (GMAT) or the Graduate Record Exam (GRE), and letters of recommendation from professors or other reputable personal connections. Graduate business courses for an MBA in digital media management may include accounting, finance, marketing, management, information systems, and digital technologies.

Other universities offer programs specific to social media. These include

A video journalist records a musician during a performance. Video journalism, television, and photo journalism coursework in undergraduate and graduate programs can offer career paths to becoming a social media manager.

West Virginia University's master of science degree in integrated marketing communications and the University of Florida's master of arts degree in social media. These programs are structured learning frameworks that can sometimes be taken online.

INTERNSHIPS

Internships can help people determine their major area of study or start them on a career path. An intern is a student or graduate gaining supervised practical experience in a real work environment. Internships are temporary positions that offer on-the-job training within a company. They are usually unpaid. Many internships offer course credit for those who are enrolled in an academic program. The experience obtained in an internship is an invaluable benefit for students and graduates. Students can work on various skills, such as leadership, writing, and social media expertise, while being supervised and trained by professionals. This experience is particularly helpful for finding a first job out of school.

The *New York Times* published statistics from a study involving postings from September 2015 to October 2016 about the most popular fields for internships. These fields included business operations, marketing, engineering, sales and business development, media, communications and public relations, and project management, among others. The study also listed the "most in-demand skills" that were needed for each of these fields. Many employers were looking for interns that had social media experience or social media education. Two of the top five fields (marketing ranked second and media, communications, and public relations ranked fifth) were interested in interns who had social media experience.

CERTIFICATION PROGRAMS

An effective way to boost one's credentials when seeking a job as a social media manager is to complete a certification program. An employer that hires a person who has certification assumes that the individual has the appropriate qualifications to perform a certain job or task. For example, there are certification programs available in digital and internet marketing. Subjects in these programs include

This mind map illustrates the elements required in digital marketing. Completing a certification program can help a social media manager gain credibility in the eyes of employers because certain skills and areas of expertise—such as in digital marketing—have been proven.

social media networking strategies, analytics, interactive marketing methods, and strategies for integrating social media into an organization or company.

Programs teach people specific techniques and best practices for specific platforms and the different approaches people have taken for their social media plans. Business goals and strategies are often discussed in addition to teaching students how to use the various tools offered by social media sites, including Radian6, Viralheat, Hootsuite, Klout, and Twittalyzer. There are many programs to investigate, both online and in a traditional classroom, for those who are looking to target social media management as a career. They are not all equal, so carefully research programs that dovetail well with your chosen career path.

chapter 4

STARTING A CAREER

Education is the first part of pursuing a career in social media. The next step is actually starting one's career. There are several options available to people interested in social media management. Some choose to work for themselves by starting their own practice. Others choose to work for a company and manage its social media accounts. Researching which companies need social media managers can help job candidates focus on finding the right fit for their interests and skills.

CREATING A PORTFOLIO

Many professionals and hiring managers recommend that those looking for work in social media have a portfolio to share during the interview and hiring process. A portfolio is a collection of creative work that showcases a person's abilities and skills to a potential employer.

What should go into a social media manager's portfolio? A common recommendation is to include screenshots of any previous social media work. These could be screenshots of tweets that were part of an advertising campaign. Another example is a screenshot of a blog post that was written in support of a brand. Any special campaign sample is worth including in a portfolio. A portfolio should contain a lengthy example of content along with a sampling of brief social posts to illustrate the

A career portfolio is a useful way to provide hiring managers with a quick look into a person's accomplishments and creative style.

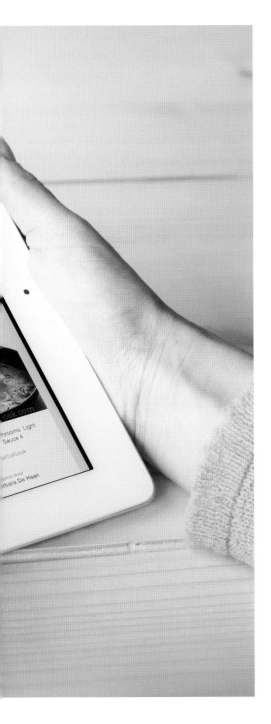

person's writing style. Finally, reports and analyses of previous social media work the person has performed also should be included. Most employers like to see how effective a person's earlier work was on the job.

Social media managers should expect potential employers to examine their social media accounts. The employers will want to see how these people conduct themselves online. Offensive or objectionable posts hurt a person's chances of landing the desired job. However, if candidates show that they can handle themselves in a professional way online, they will make themselves look more attractive as possible employees. Besides managing a company's brand, social media managers must demonstrate that they can handle their own personal "brands" competently.

There are steps people can take to improve their social media presence. First, they should clean up so-called digital dirt. View any social media accounts from an employer's point of view. Tweets, posts, and images that could be seen as being objectionable should be removed. These could be tweets with inappropriate words or embarrassing photos posted by friends. The next step is to build an online profile using established platforms such as LinkedIn and Facebook. LinkedIn, in particular, is popular for professionals and can act as an online résumé. In addition, professional versions of different accounts should be set up. For instance, people should create professional accounts on Facebook besides their personal accounts, which always should be kept private.

STARTING A PRIVATE PRACTICE

One option for social media managers who want to be their own bosses is to start private practices. There are pros and cons of setting up one's own business. It can be rewarding to be one's own boss, but it can also be stressful, and success can be inconsistent. There are several steps to take to begin a private practice.

The first step is to establish an online presence. This process is similar to creating an online portfolio and various professional social media accounts. It can also be a great way to familiarize oneself with the platforms that are popular at the moment. In addition, those working on their own should set up a website to represent their businesses.

Next, the person needs to find clients. This step can be challenging and sometimes frustrating. The independent business owner must learn where ideal clients spend their time online. Then start conversations in those locations and try to drive traffic to one's professional website. Another place to meet clients is at conferences, events, and networking functions. Landing just one influential client could be a turning point toward success. A person with his or her own practice

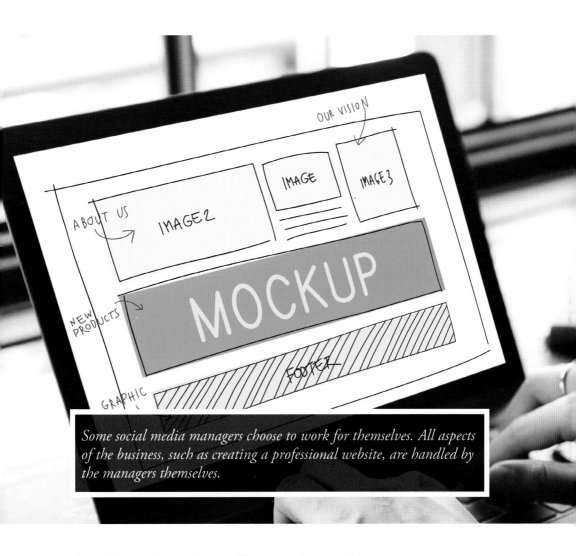

Some social media managers choose to work for themselves. All aspects of the business, such as creating a professional website, are handled by the managers themselves.

should combine these efforts with an advertising strategy to have a sound business plan.

One matter to think about is how much one should charge clients for services. Find out what competitors are charging, and then decide whether it would be best to charge more or less than them.

WHO NEEDS A SOCIAL MEDIA MANAGER?

Which companies need a social media manager? Determining who is hiring for the job is a pivotal step when beginning a career. A company must first be able to afford a social media manager. Smaller companies usually do not have the money in their budgets for a full-time social media employee.

Companies that seem unresponsive to requests and comments online may need a social media manager. Customers expect a quick response. A social media manager directly addresses this need for fast feedback. A social media manager should be able to identify when a company's social media presence and brand are falling behind its competitors. Reaching out to the company to present one's expertise and usefulness is another way a social media manager could find a position. Tracking down a company that is investing a lot of money in advertising is another approach to becoming a prospective social media manager.

APPLYING

There are many websites that are dedicated to posting job openings. Sites such as Monster and ZipRecruiter connect job seekers with employers. There are also sites that concentrate on media and marketing jobs. A site like Mediabistro caters to jobs in publishing and other media, including social media, and offers training courses and résumé services. Sites such as CareerBuilder or Indeed generally have job postings from all industries, including sales and information technology.

Applying for jobs and open positions is now mostly an online pursuit with the introduction of online job boards, career-oriented mobile applications, and employment-related search engines.

As previously noted, social media managers can sometimes have vague job titles such as link builder or community manager. These jobs often perform the same job tasks as that of social media manager but are trickier to discover when doing a general search online. It is vital to search different job titles related to the field of social media. Focusing on a job's requirements or duties might provide more search results.

ELLA W. HERNANDEZ
(214) 555-5555
ellawhernandez@emailaddress.com
LinkedIn | Facebook | Twitter Name | Snapchat Name | Skype: EllaSkypeName

SOCIAL MEDIA MANAGER
Marketing professional with 2+ years of experience in social media management, content marketing, and advertising. Earned a BA in journalism with expertise in web development. Excellent communication, copywriting, and brand awareness skills.

EDUCATION
• Master of Business Administration: State University
  Specialization: Social Media Advertising
• Bachelor of Arts: University of the United States
  Major: Journalism

EXPERIENCE
Social Media Coordinator, Daisy's Donuts, Mesquite, TX   April 2015–February 2017
• Wrote, updated, and maintained content for web and mobile sites
• Developed online marketing campaigns
• Drove brand awareness
• Monitored online presence of company's brand
• Engaged with users, strengthening customer relationships
• Supported user generation

Product Marketing Manager, CyberCompany, Carol Stream, IL   May 2013–March 2015
• Managed national products
• Supported sales channel to achieve 100 percent of revenue goals
• Contributed to the company's social media strategy
• Launched the company's first mobile applications

SKILLS AND TOOLS

• Adobe CQ	• HTC Vive	• Reddit
• Audacity	• HTML	• Snapchat
• CSS	• InDesign	• Twitter
• Dreamweaver	• Instagram	• Wikipedia
• Facebook	• LinkedIn	• WordPress
• Flickr	• MySpace	• XML
• Google Analytics	• Pinterest	• YouTube

REFERNCES
Available on request

An example of a résumé for a social media manager is shown here. Successful résumés clearly and succinctly detail the applicant's experience and skills that can be useful to a company.

Professionals suggest networking and connecting with people who hold the type of position a job candidate is seeking. This contact can be a good way to find out about news in the field and keep current with the industry's trends. The connections can also lead job seekers to potential job openings. Alternatively, job seekers can have potential employers come to them. Someone who creates an impressive online presence could have interested companies contacting him or her to make a job offer.

New job seekers should not expect to land a dream job immediately. Most people have to work their way up to where they really want to be in a company's hierarchy. Entry-level positions are the first step toward a successful career. A social media coordinator is an entry-level position, for example. That person creates content to post online and helps manage online conversations. The social media coordinator often assists more experienced members of the social media team.

INTERVIEWING

After successfully applying for a social media manager position, employers will bring in candidates for interviews. It has become standard to have multiple interviews for a position. The process usually begins with an initial phone call, then a face-to-face meeting, and perhaps a prescreening test along with additional meetings with higher-level managers and executives. When reviewing candidates, interviewers will try to determine if the person is really interested in the work of the company. They will also want to know if the job candidate treats colleagues as equals, no matter what position those people hold within the organization.

Employers will quickly eliminate candidates based on what they see on a résumé. Companies can sometimes receive hundreds of applications for open positions. Interviewers do not

Interviewing Tips

The questions that a candidate for a social media position encounters in an interview usually fall within four categories. One category is general knowledge about social media. These questions are meant to see if a person has a certain level of knowledge about social media and networking. Some of those questions are: What social media tools are you familiar with? What are your strengths and weaknesses in social media? How have you increased your knowledge about social media?

Dressing professionally for a job interview can foster confidence in the hiring manager that you will conduct yourself like a professional if you are hired for the position.

Questions could also be about the social media industry to find out how involved in the field a prospective hire is. These are more specific and meant to test how up to date someone is regarding technology. Employers might ask candidates to explain a new technology, such as Web 2.0, or the latest social media platforms and social media networking sites. Candidates might be asked about the blogs and sites that they read and follow or whom they admire in the social media industry.

Other questions are more technical. These are designed to determine a person's level of technical knowledge. For example, what is the difference between a Facebook "like" and a "share"? Or, how frequently should various accounts be updated? Similarly, questions may try to determine how much a person knows about analytics and marketing. Questions in this category include how to determine ROI or how a social media campaign begins and ends.

Finally, a company might ask an interviewee about the specific company. The interviewer want to find out if the person has the proper skills to improve its social media team. Questions might be asked about what strategies the company should pursue or which social media sites they should invest in.

want to waste their time with unqualified candidates. These prequalifications vary from company to company. Many are the skills previously mentioned in this resource. Experience will also be taken into consideration. Having had an internship in the field can really help a candidate who is fresh out of school get a leg up on the competition.

chapter 5

Advancing in Social Media Management

How can a social media manager cultivate success? There are things a social media manager can do to prove his or her value to the company. After all, companies must show that their investment in an employee is paying off. A social media manager is indeed an investment and that person must demonstrate that the company was correct in pursuing a social media strategy in its business plan.

Set Clear Objectives

An employee's tasks and goals are usually set by a direct manager or upper-level management. These people are the leaders who decide what the company and their individual teams will concentrate their efforts on. However, some social media managers are given a little more power in deciding what should be their day-to-day focus. A social media manager needs to take advantage of the times he or she is given an opportunity to set a goal or objective. For instance, a manager might ask for ideas about how an upcoming product campaign should be run.

According to an article on the social media marketing site Krusecontrolinc.com, there are common challenges a business faces regarding social media. One challenge is low web traffic. A clear objective could be to increase traffic by some number or percentage such as by one thousand visitors per day or by 25

Setting clear objectives and goals can help an employee grow in the job and progress in a social media management career. Working well with and proving value to one's manager can lead to acquiring additional responsibilities.

percent. Another challenge might be the company's weak brand awareness. A goal could be to create more company mentions on Twitter. Other problems include declining customer retention, poor online reputation, and slow sales. Objectives must create results that are clear and obtainable. There should be no question about when they are attained or when results fall short.

PROOF OF VALUE

Setting clear objectives is a great way to provide proof of the value one can bring to a company. Similar to how businesses use ROIs to look at how they are spending resources, social media managers can show their own ROI. They must show that their work generates tangible results. This validation is done by measuring and analyzing key numbers for which a social media manager is responsible. Monitor and keep track of these results to understand performance quality daily.

Crucial numbers or indicators, as have been reported by Krusecontrolinc .com, include audience growth, audience profile, audience engagement, response rate, and negative feedback. Different companies value some indicators more than others. Determining which ones are valued by the company is a major step. Once the indicators have been chosen, measuring them should become a standard part of the job.

Numbers on their own are not quite enough to prove one's value to a company. The related data should be given an appropriate presentation. One popular option is to create an infographic that displays data in a visual display. For example, data about the most successful campaigns can be turned into a series of charts and images that present the positive results of one's hard work.

Proof of a social media manager's monetary value to the company can be shown using charts, graphs, and tables that display data showing the success of the projects and social media campaigns the manager ran.

Another way to show a social media manager's value is to collect testimonials. A testimonial is a recommendation given by a former employer, client, or coworker. Sites such as LinkedIn include testimonials on profile pages. Personal recommendations are a more emotional proof of value than data and numbers. They can leave a positive impression on supervisors and employers and provide reasons to believe in someone.

EXCEEDING EXPECTATIONS

To advance in the field, one should exceed expectations, or go above and beyond what people expect from the role. For instance, there can be times when something goes very wrong at a business. How the social media manager handles the situation can go a long way in furthering that person's reputation at work. When it comes time to reward employees, the person who stayed calm in the middle of a catastrophe is usually seen as more capable than the person who lost control during the crisis.

One way to surpass expectations is to create a memorable and positive customer experience. A customer who makes contact through a business's social media accounts might want a problem resolved. After the issue is addressed, the social media manager could do something special for the customer. Not only will the customer be grateful, but anyone who sees the special treatment will remember it, too.

WORKING ONE'S WAY UP

Moving up in the social media hierarchy means earning a title such as social media director or another that signifies a specific management level. These roles are more about deciding strategy and less about posting status updates and content. Job tasks, of course, depend on an employer's demands. Choosing

REAL WORLD LESSONS

The social media and marketing manager for a dessert franchise shared a few helpful tips learned on the job. The position required running the shop's many social media accounts, including Instagram, Facebook, and Twitter.

One lesson was that building hype before a new product or location launches is important, but there is the possibility of doing too much. The manager posted three posts per day before there was even an opening date for a new dessert store location, and eventually the followers protested about being baited about the products that weren't even available yet. Another lesson was that businesses must be able to handle negative feedback from customers. Reviews are not always positive, so customer disapproval must be used as constructive criticism.

The dessert company's social media and marketing manager also learned that paying extra for Facebook exposure, for "boosted posts," was a great way to reach more people and connect with possible customers. Another advantage was that photographs of attractive dessert products were perfect for posting on Instagram.

which other social media accounts to follow or like on Facebook or Twitter is typically the job of those who work below management level. Management decides instead on how to promote a product or service. Higher-level social media positions can also involve researching competitors and determining how to raise brand awareness.

Management roles need the same skills as entry-level positions. However, more experience in social media project management is required. Only those who have demonstrated a high skill level in creating content, writing, communicating, and using social media and analytic tools are considered for the top positions in managing a team. Top managers must also show an ability to quickly adapt to the industry and its newest trends. For example, SEO became a very important part of social media around 2010. The way search engines display results, though, has changed since then. If social media managers are still using the strategy that worked in 2010 today, then they will quickly discover that they are falling behind their competitors. Finally, having experience managing a pivotal project will enable someone to move into management. Combining solid experience with proven skills can usually lead to advancement.

RELATED JOBS

Sometimes moving forward in one's career requires taking a similar job on the same level. This job change is called a lateral move. Keeping an eye on promising job opportunities in social media management is a good strategy when making a lateral move.

SOCIAL MEDIA STRATEGIST

One similar job title to social media manager is social media strategist. A person in this position helps decide on the specifics for a marketing campaign and then tracks the campaign's progress. For example, a social media strategist may need to choose which platform should be used in a new advertising campaign. That person could choose Twitter, and the tweets could be written to encourage followers to visit the company's online store. As the campaign is put into action, the social media strategist will then monitor the traffic on the company's store website. The person in this position could also be responsible for maintaining social media sites and accounts and meeting with clients to create a social media action plan.

To become a social media strategist, job candidates must have a bachelor's degree. Recommended majors are communications, journalism, or marketing. It is extremely helpful for social media strategists to have writing and computer skills. The US Bureau of Labor Statistics (BLS) predicts a promising future for those working as social media strategists. The BLS estimates that employment for this job category will increase by 9 percent from 2014 to 2024.

SOCIAL MEDIA SALES REPRESENTATIVE

In another area of the social media industry is the social media sales representative. A sales representative's job is to find new clients. Social media sales representatives find people or businesses that are interested in using social media to increase their brand's awareness. This position's role is very similar to that of someone starting a private practice. Finding new clients can involve attending social media events or cold-calling various companies. (A cold call is visiting or making a phone call to a potential customer to attempt to sell that person something without being asked by the customer to do so.) Social media sales representatives also meet with current clients to talk about new plans for using social media in advertising.

The BLS expects that employment for social media sales representatives will decline by 3 percent from 2014 to 2024. People performing this job could see their responsibilities evolve over time. Candidates for a social media sales representative position must have a bachelor's degree. Recommended majors include communications, journalism, or marketing. Additional requirements are writing and computer skills.

Setting up in-person meetings with potential business customers can be an important method in selling a product or service. A social media sales representative needs to have good communication skills with people at all levels of an organization.

OTHER POSITIONS

There are many other possible positions for lateral movement involving social media. Job titles include digital marketing manager, content marketing manager, customer experience manager, and community manager, among others. Companies call these and similar roles by a variety of names. Job seekers in this field need to determine what these roles' responsibilities are so that they can find the right fit for them.

chapter 6

A FUTURE IN SOCIAL MEDIA

The social media industry's rise over the past decade has been impressive. It will no doubt continue to evolve. How will social media managers' jobs change? There are many examples of how social media managers are adjusting to the challenges they face today. What lessons have today's online marketers learned that can be useful for tomorrow's social media managers?

MOVING FORWARD

Marketing firms are at the forefront of social media. Paying attention to how they approach their clients' challenges is a valuable way to recognize the trends in social media. From these trends, it is possible to gauge where the industry is headed. For example, one marketing firm noted that social visualization is changing the strategy of what content to publish. People are reacting more to images than they are to text posts and tweets. This trend was supported by Twitter when it launched TwitPic in 2008. Furthermore, Pinterest, a platform heavy on graphics, was the fastest-growing network in 2014. Social media managers must sharpen their graphic design skills to survive in the industry.

Along the same lines, video has become a major form of content. Periscope, a live-video sharing application, was launched by Twitter in 2015 to capture the video-watching audience. YouTube has more than one billion users and Snapchat, which debuted on the stock market in 2017, quickly earned more than one billion dollars for its founders. Reaching

Video is increasingly becoming an essential part of social media. Numerous mobile apps such as YouTube and Periscope make sharing live video effortless for social media managers.

a wider audience will require a social media manager with strong skills in video communication.

One trend gaining momentum is being mobile friendly. This means having a website or application that can be easily

visited or used on a smartphone or tablet. A study by online marketers predicted that 25 percent of all sales made online by 2017 would be made through a smartphone or other mobile device. Businesses used to think of mobile-friendly sites as less important than traditional websites that are made for desktop or laptop computers. But today companies see mobile-friendly websites as being vital for sales. Google has changed the way it ranks search results, too. Sites that are mobile friendly are given higher priority in the Google rankings. Businesses are now designing their websites to be responsive to mobile demands. Consequently, the website can be displayed in different ways depending on the device a person is using.

PROFESSIONAL TIPS FROM A SOCIAL MEDIA MANAGER

According to the US Department of Labor, social media positions will increase the number of public

STAYING FLEXIBLE

Technology is always changing. Social media managers must pay attention to how their industry is adapting or risk losing potential customers. In 2013, Facebook changed the algorithm that decided which posts appear on a user's page or timeline. Companies that had gotten used to the way Facebook chose content suddenly had to revise their strategies.

Another change occurred when Google amended its search engine algorithms. What used to work for companies no longer did. That change brought about many new strategies to increase sales by content marketers and social media managers. Social media managers must be able to quickly adapt to the constant changes in technology.

relations jobs by 12 percent by the year 2020. In 2014, the popular job listings feature on LinkedIn showed that there were more than three thousand open social media manager positions, while CareerBuilder listed another five thousand positions. If the current trends continue, these numbers will only increase over time.

Despite research showing that the industry will grow stronger in the coming years, some professionals believe that social media jobs will fade away. They believe that employees in other job roles will learn how to use social media. This could mean that people who focus solely on social media will no longer be hired. Another way to look at it is that instead of disappearing, social media managers will evolve. They must add more abilities to their skill set.

Industry professionals believe that social media managers must learn to use content marketing. Content marketing is the practice of publishing different forms of content to keep the

To improve products and service, social media managers need to learn about the likes and dislikes of their companies' customers. A social media manager at a restaurant, for example, should become familiar with the offerings on the menu and what customers prefer by becoming aware of what they write online about their restaurant experience.

attention of a certain audience. The goal is to attract more people to a particular business or product. Social media managers are therefore encouraged to learn how to be a successful content marketer. Becoming a superior writer and communicator is beneficial to social media managers who need to adapt on the job. Other valuable skills include a grasp of advanced SEO knowledge, analytics technology, and mass emailing systems.

Social media managers can also learn to focus more on customers. They must know how to listen to what their company's customers are saying and what it is they want. For example, a social media manager at a restaurant could learn about the different dishes the customers like and dislike. Then, he or she could take the findings to whoever oversees the menu. There should be someone paying attention to what customers want. Social media managers are in the perfect position to do that.

SOCIAL MEDIA CHALLENGES

Working with a business's customers and clients requires skill and patience. A small issue can grow into something serious. For example, if a customer service representative treats a customer badly, that customer can then influence other customers to avoid that business by posting negative comments online. On social media, where it is easy to reach a large audience, the complicated challenges of working with customers are even more apparent. Upsetting a single customer can become a national news story, especially for large businesses with a huge customer base.

This challenge became a reality for the restaurant chain Wendy's in early 2017. One of Wendy's main marketing points is that the restaurants never freeze the meat that is used for their hamburgers. A person on Twitter challenged this idea, claiming that Wendy's does, in fact, freeze the meat. After a few exchanges on Twitter, the Wendy's social media manager seemed to have the accusation and situation under control, defending the company in a conversational tone that many people found entertaining. Then the social media manager posted a tweet that some found offensive. It was an image of Pepe the Frog, an internet meme whose meaning has evolved over time. The meme had grown in popularity with the controversial white nationalist movement and became associated with racism and hate. The social media manager who sent the tweet was unfamiliar with how that meme's meaning had changed. With a single tweet of the hate symbol dressed as the restaurant's mascot, Wendy's reputation took a massive negative hit.

The company quickly deleted the tweet and responded with an explanation of the situation, but the damage had been done. Social media managers must pay attention to internet trends to avoid situations such as these. Understanding that the entire context of the content they publish and share is crucial and can directly affect sales and the company's bottom line.

TOMORROW'S SOCIAL MEDIA INDUSTRY

Social media today may not look like social media tomorrow. Those in the industry have several predictions for what it will look like in the near future. Instead of multiple platforms, the future could see just one major social media platform that everyone uses. For instance, there was a time when there were many search engines available to internet users. Although there are still options available, most people now use Google. In the same way, Facebook could become the dominant social media platform. The company has already added Instagram to its holdings and could add more platforms in the future. Or the sole social media platform could be a new company that does not even exist today. Regardless, the all-in-one social experience is a possibility. This alternative could be taken a step further in a situation in which this single platform offers users a number of services, such as shopping or ordering food.

Companies today can have their content appear on a user's page, such as a Facebook feed, alongside content posted by that user's friends and family members. In the future, this could be more difficult as social media platforms feature more content from users. A clothing store, for instance, could have a story about its new designs appear in Facebook's timeline feature today. But soon, it could have to pay a lot more money to have that same visibility.

According to Jayson DeMers's article about the future of social media marketing on Marketingland.com, other possibilities for social media include individualization, niche segmentation, and virtual and augmented reality. In

New technology can change what works in social media management. An apparel shop in Japan uses augmented reality technology to show customers how they would look in various clothing styles. Customers can then post photos on social media to request feedback from friends and family members.

individualization, users will have more control over what they can and cannot see on their news feed pages. Businesses will have to learn new ways to reach their potential customers. In niche segmentation, which is the opposite of the all-in-one

social media platform, users will be able to send their images and videos privately with customizations. Some in the industry believe that there could be even more platforms available to users. Each of these platforms will focus on one small part of social media, such as images on one platform and videos on another. Virtual reality is growing in popularity and is providing users with a different way to experience their surrounding world and share it via social media. Augmented reality is a real-world environment that has been supplemented by computer-generated sound, video, graphics, and global positioning system information. Marketers hope to be using augmented reality in retail advertising. Journalist Jennifer Gregory explained on IBM.com how augmented reality might work. Fashion businesses could use augmented reality to show potential customers how clothing might look and fit on them without the customers having to go to a store to try it on. A customer would upload a selfie into an app and then choose the items to virtually try on. The app shows the item on the selfie so the customer can see how it looks on him or her. Then the customer can share the photo with friends or family members on social media to solicit feedback.

Social media is undeniably a part of everyday life in the modern world. Millions of people make daily visits to one of the many popular sites online that allow them to share photos, post their thoughts, and connect with friends and family members. With so many people congregating online and exchanging ideas, businesses have taken notice. Business is conducted differently today than it was even ten years ago. How it will evolve in the next ten years will be an exciting thing to watch, and social media managers will have front-row seats.

glossary

brand The unique combination of designs, symbols, and words that businesses use to identify their products and services as being different from their competitors.

campaign A linked series of activities that are designed to be used in marketing a new or changed product or service.

certification A designation that assures employers that a person has achieved the qualifications to perform a certain job or task.

infographic A chart, graph, or other image presenting information in a visual form.

integrated marketing communications A style of marketing through an organized use of various promotional methods that are planned to reinforce one another.

marketing funnel A system that assists in tracking the stages a potential customer travels through in deciding to purchase a product or service.

meme An image, video, or text that is copied and spread rapidly by internet users.

mobile friendly When a website can easily be used on the small screens of mobile devices, such as smartphones or tablets.

objectionable Offensive; arousing a feeling of disapproval.

objective An aim or goal.

podcast A digital audio or video file or recording, usually part of a series, that can be downloaded from the internet.

portfolio A collection of creative work that shows a person's abilities and skills to a potential employer.

prescreening The practice of examining before further selection processes occur for interviews.

retention The act of keeping possession or use of something.

return on investment (ROI) The measure of the gain or loss made on an investment relative to its cost. The formula typically used to calculate ROI is ROI equals the gain from the investment minus the cost of the investment divided by the cost of the investment. It is usually expressed as a percentage.

revenue Income generated by an investment.

soft selling Selling something using subtlety, friendliness, and low-pressure tactics.

tangible Being able to be perceived as real and verifiable.

trait A quality or characteristic that makes one person or thing different from another.

for more information

American Marketing Association (AMA)
4400 Massachusetts Avenue NW
Washington, DC 20016
(855) 725-7614
Website: https://www.ama.org
Facebook: @AmericanMarketing
Twitter: @AMA_Marketing
LinkedIn: @american-marketing-association
The AMA offers news about the latest in marketing and connects marketing professionals with one another. Its website offers a career page with an online applications process.

Bureau of Labor Statistics (BLS)
US Department of Labor
2 Massachusetts Avenue NE, PSB Suite 2135
Washington, DC 20212-0001
(202) 691-5700
Website: https://www.bls.gov
Twitter: @BLS_gov
The BLS's *Occupational Outlook Handbook* (https://www .bls.gov/ooh) helps readers find information such as training requirements, responsibilities, tasks, and average salaries for various careers and occupations.

Canadian Internet Marketing Association (CIMA)
Email: web@internetmarketingassociation.ca
Website: http://www.internetmarketingassociation.ca
Facebook: @Canadian-Internet-Marketing-Association-CIMA
LinkedIn: @Canadian-Internet-Marketing-Association
The CIMA provides resources and training to marketing pro-

fessionals and members of the public.

Canadian Marketing Association (CMA)
1 Concorde Gate, Suite 607
Don Mills, ON M3C 3N6
Canada
(800) 267-8805
Fax: 416-441-4062
Email: info@theCMA.ca
Website: https://www.the-cma.org
Facebook: @Cdnmarketing
Twitter: @Cdnmarketing
The CMA sponsors events and provides education for profes-
   sionals and businesses looking to improve their marketing
   strategies. Its website offers a career resources page.

Schools.com
950 Tower Lane, Sixth Floor
Foster City, California 94404
Website: http://www.schools.com/visuals/how-to-become-a
   -social-media-marketing-specialist.html
Facebook: @Schoolscom
Twitter: @schoolsedu
Schools.com is an online resource for students who are interested in various careers. The site provides information
   about degree programs and schools, including those for
   people interested in pursuing the career path of a social
   media marketing specialist.

Social Media Association
130 Shore Road, Suite 146
Port Washington, NY 11050
(631) 393-0220
Website: http://socialmediaassoc.com

Facebook: @socialmediaassociation
Twitter: @SoMeAssociation
LinkedIn: @social-media-association
Instagram: @someassocli
The Social Media Association brings professionals together online and at their events to discuss social, digital, and future media.

WEBSITES

Because of the changing nature of internet links, Rosen Publishing has developed an online list of websites related to the subject of this book. This site is updated regularly. Please use this link to access the list:

http://www.rosenlinks.com/ECAR/Social

for further reading

Earl, C. F. *Building a Business in the Virtual World*. Broomall, PA: Mason Crest Publishers, 2014.

Furgang, Kathy. *20 Great Career-Building Activities Using Twitter*. New York, NY: Rosen Publishing, 2017.

Henneberg, Susan. *20 Great Career-Building Activities Using Tumblr*. New York, NY: Rosen Publishing, 2017.

Kerpen, Dave. *Likeable Social Media: How to Delight Your Customers, Create an Irresistible Brand, and Be Amazing on Facebook, Twitter, LinkedIn, Instagram, Pinterest, and More.* Rev. ed. New York, NY: McGraw Hill Education, 2015.

Marsh, Carole. *Job Tracks: 60 Great Careers and How to Get from Where You Are ... To Where You Want to Go!* Peachtree City, GA: Gallopade International, 2012.

Nichols, Susan. *Cool Careers Without College for People Who Love Tech*. New York, NY: Rosen Publishing, 2017.

Pawlewski, Sarah. *Careers: The Graphic Guide to Finding the Perfect Job for You*. New York, NY: DK Publishing, 2015.

Rauf, Don. *Getting Paid to Manage Social Media*. New York, NY: Rosen Publishing, 2017.

Small, Cathleen. *20 Great Career-Building Activities Using Facebook*. New York, NY: Rosen Publishing, 2017.

Spilsbury, Richard. *I'm Good at Media—What Job Can I Get?* London, UK: Wayland, 2013.

Steffens, Bradley. *Careers in Internet Technology*. San Diego, CA: ReferencePoint Press, Inc., 2017.

bibliography

Ayres, Scott. "How to Become a Social Media Manager in 6 Simple Steps." Post Planner. Retrieved February 8, 2017. https://www.postplanner.com/how-to-become-a-social-media-manager-in-6-steps.

Blanchard, Olivier. *Social Media ROI: Managing and Measuring Social Media Efforts in Your Organization.* Indianapolis, IN: Que, 2011.

Briz, Brooks, and David Rose. *Getting a Social Media Job for Dummies.* Hoboken, NJ: John Wiley & Sons, 2015.

Bunch, Eric. "The Evolution of Social Media Marketing: 9 Trends to Know Now." August 31, 2015. http://docplayer.net/10430634-The-evolution-of-social-media-marketing-9-trends-to-know-now.html.

Carlson, Nicholas. "Facebook Slightly Tweaked How the Site Works—And It Screwed an Entire Profession." Business Insider, December 13, 2013. http://www.businessinsider.com/facebook-screws-social-media-marketers-2013-12.

Claveria, Kelvin. "The Social Media Manager Is (Almost) Dead: 5 Tips on How to Evolve as A Marketer——#MyIndustry." LinkedIn, March 27, 2014. https://www.linkedin.com/ pulse/20140327143305-45997570-the-social-media-manager-is-almost-dead-5-tips-on-how-to-evolve-as-a-marketer-myindustry.

DeMers, Jayson. "5 Skills Your Social Media Manager Must Have." *Forbes*, June 8, 2015. https://www.forbes.com/sites/jaysondemers/2015/06/08/5-skills-your-social-media-manager-must-have/#116d7427ac56.

DeMers, Jayson. "6 Possibilities for the Future of Social Media Marketing." Marketing Land, August 22, 2016.

http://marketingland.com/6-possibilities-future-social
-media-marketing-188391.

Duboff, Josh. "Who's Really Pulling the Strings on Stars'
Social-Media Accounts." Vanities. *Vanity Fair*, September
8, 2016. http://www.vanityfair.com/style/2016/09
/celebrity-social-media-accounts.

Education Life: The List. "Top 20 Fields for Internships:
Get Your Skills On." *New York Times*, February 3, 2017.
https://www.nytimes.com/2017/02/03/education/edlife
/top-20-fields-for-internships-get-your-skills-on.html.

Farr, Amy. "5 Signs You Need to Hire a Social Media Manager." SEMrush Blog, September 17, 2015. https://www
.semrush.com/blog/5-signs-you-need-to-hire-a-social
-media-manager.

Fischer, Kristen. "How to Get a Job in Social Media." Mediabistro, March 8, 2016. https://www.mediabistro.com
/get-hired/job-search/what-every-job-seeker-should-know
-about-landing-social-media-jobs.

Gregory, Jennifer. "Augmented Reality and Virtual Reality:
The Next Frontier in Social Media Marketing. THINK
Marketing, November 8, 2016. https://www.ibm.com
/think/marketing/augmented-reality-and-virtual-reality
-the-next-frontier-in-social-media-marketing.

Hendricks, Drew. "Do You Need a Social Media Manager?
6 Questions to Ask Yourself." *Forbes*, October 10, 2014.
http://www.forbes.com/sites/drewhendricks/2014/10/10
/do-you-need-a-social-media-manager-6-questions-to-ask
-yourself/#17ba3adb2154.

Jones, Beth. "What Does a Social Media Manager Actually
Do?" *Social Media Success Magazine*, August 4, 2015.
http://socialmediasuccessmagazine.com/blog/what-does-a
-social-media-manager-actually-do.

Klososky, Scott. *Manager's Guide to Social Media*. New York,
NY: McGraw-Hill, 2011.

Kruse Control. "Social Media Manager Job Description: A Complete Guide." May 2, 2016. https://www .krusecontrolinc.com/social-media-manager-job -description-complete-guide.

Low, Amanda Layman. "6 Secrets to Success as a Social Media Manager." Mediabistro, January 27, 2016. https://www .mediabistro.com/climb-the-ladder/skills-expertise/6 -secrets-to-success-as-a-social-media-manager.

Martin, James A. "10 Top Social Media Marketing Success Stories." CIO, April 28, 2016. http://www.cio.com /article/3062615/social-networking/10-top-social-media -marketing-success-stories.html#slide3.

McHugh, Kenna. "10 Qualities of a Successful Social Media Manager." *Adweek*, September 28, 2011. http://www .adweek.com/digital/10-qualities-of-a-successful-social -media-manager.

Muckensturm, Elizabeth. "The Growth of the Social Media Manager as a Career." EnVeritas Group, April 14, 2014. https://enveritasgroup.com/campfire/social-media -manager-as-a-career.

Phillips, Beth. "Curriculum for a High School Social Media Class." JEADigitalMediaorg, August 23, 2012. http:// www.jeadigitalmedia.org/2012/08/23/curriculum-for-a -high-school-social-media-class.

Prish, Stan. "Top 69 Social Media Job Interview Questions." LinkedIn, January 30, 2015. https://www.linkedin.com /pulse/top-69-social-media-job-interview-questions -stan-prish.

Professional & Continuing Education, University of Washington. "Certificate in Social Media Technologies and Implementation: Engage Your Audience Through Diverse Social Media Platforms." Retrieved February 6, 2017. https://www.pce.uw.edu/certificates/social-media -technologies-implementation.

Shein, Esther. "Social Media Goes to School." Scholastic.com.
    Retrieved February 6, 2017. http://www.scholastic.com
    /browse/article.jsp?id=3758300.

Spoon University. "What I Learned from Working as a Social
    Media Manager for a Dessert Shop." Huffington Post, July
    19, 2016. http://www.huffingtonpost.com/spoon
    -university/what-i-learned-from-working-as-a-social
    -media-manager-for-a-bake-shop_b_11070340.html.

Story, Mark. *Starting Your Career as a Social Media Manager.*
    New York, NY: Allworth Press, 2012.

Study.com. "Social Media Careers: Education Requirements
    and Job Info." Retrieved February 4, 2017. http://study
    .com/articles/Social_Media_Careers_Education
    _Requirements_and_Job_Info.html.

Torpey, Elka. "Social Media Specialist: Career Outlook." US
    Bureau of Labor Statistics. Retrieved February 4, 2017.
    https://www.bls.gov/careeroutlook/2016/youre-a-what
    /social-media-specialist.htm.

WeRSM—We Are Social Media, guest blogger. "Why You
    Should Have a Portfolio If You Work in Social Media."
    November 20, 2014. http://wersm.com/why-you-should
    -have-a-portfolio-if-you-work-in-social-media.

Whitten, Sarah. "A Wendy's Tweet Just Went Viral for All the
    Wrong Reasons." CNBC, January 4, 2017. http://www
    .cnbc.com/2017/01/04/wendys-saucy-tweets-are-hit-and
    -miss-on-social-media.html.

index

ABOUT THE AUTHOR

Jeff Mapua is the author of several books, including *A Career in Customer Service and Tech Support*, *Net Neutrality and What It Means to You*, and *Coping with Cyberbullying*. He has professional experience working on social media campaigns and content marketing for national and global companies. Mapua lives in Dallas, Texas, with his wife, Ruby.

PHOTO CREDITS:

Cover, p. 1 (figure) Neustockimages/E+/Getty Images; Cover, p. 1 (background) Li Chaoshu/Shutterstock.com; pp. 4–5 Araya Diaz/Getty Images; p. 8 Vasin Lee/Shutterstock.com; pp. 10–11 The Washington Post/Getty Images; p. 12 elenabsl /Shutterstock.com; p. 15 IB Photography/Shutterstock.com; p. 19 Your Design/Shutterstock.com; pp. 20–21 Artco /Shutterstock.com; p. 23 sitthiphong/Shutterstock.com; pp. 24–25 Richard Levine/Corbis News/Getty Images; p. 30 © AP Images; pp. 32–33 Pavel L Photo and Video /Shutterstock.com; p. 35 dizain/Shutterstock.com; p. 38–39 Twin Design/Shutterstock.com; pp. 41, 49 Rawpixel.com /Shutterstock.com; p. 43 dennizn/Shutterstock.com; p. 46 Dusan Petkovic/Shutterstock.com; pp. 50–51 AndreyPopov /iStock/Thinkstock; p. 56 XiXinXing/Shutterstock.com; pp. 58–59 Brett Carlsen/Getty Images; p. 61 Dmytro Zinkevych/Shutterstock.com; pp. 64–65 Yoshikazu Tsuno /AFP/Getty Images.

Design: Matt Cauli; Layout: Tahara Anderson; Senior Editor: Kathy Kuhtz Campbell; Photo Research: Nicole DiMella